MIDNIGHT PRAYER STRATEGY

UNRAVELING THE MYSTERY

SHERENE A.P BROWN

Midnight Prayer Strategy: Unraveling the Mystery

First Edition 2023

ISBN::
Hardcover: 978-1-998245-30-7
Paperback: 978-1-998245-31-4

Cover and book design by Kabrena L. Robinson
Published by Eva-Michelle & Family Publishing
www.evamichelleandfamily.com

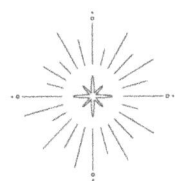

"So do not fear, for I am with you;
do not be dismayed, for I am your God.
I will strengthen you and help you;
I will uphold you with my righteous right hand."

— Isaiah 41:10

CONTENTS

ACKNOWLEDGMENT

To begin with, I want to express the profound gratitude I have for my Heavenly Father. Many years ago, He chased me and granted the anointing to write which was a prophetic event in my life. The wisdom He gave me and the nudges He used to push me on were invaluable in the process that has led to the writing and the finishing of this book.

To my immediate family and all who support me in ministry, I owe a mountain of gratitude that cannot be adequately expressed in words. Your non-stop prayers and moral support have allowed the completion of this book to come to fruition.

THE PURPOSE OF THIS BOOK

T his book is designed to alert readers to the spirituality of life. It is merely the next step in a journey of faith, partnering with God in the Great Controversy. It aims to awaken Christians to the great spiritual arsenal made available to us by God Himself, unraveling the mystery of the Midnight prayer.

In order to understand one's true purpose on earth, it is essential to understand that life is spiritual. We are spiritual beings, and Jesus' birth was spiritual. This by and large is the first mystery. Recognizing that life is spiritual means that living is also inherently spiritual. If life is spiritual, then it is nonsensical to ignore the realms of the spirit while attempting to live our lives on this earth. The spiritual is invisible and cannot be explained or equated to science.

The natural realm is a reflection of the spiritual realm.

Many unanswered questions about one's life lie in the spirit realm. The visible is gigantic, therefore the invisible is superlatively gigantic. The spiritual realm is more powerful than the natural realm hence it superimposes itself upon the natural. Events occur in the spiritual before it manifests in the natural. Believers in Christ should be able to sense the impulses of the spirit to know the speakings of God and His movements. God in His wisdom, has made provisions in each of his followers to tap into his speaking and into his responses. The summation of all these things is what the Bible refers to as discernment— simply the capacity to walk into the impulses of the Spirit.

There are many great books on the topic, each with its own approach and purpose. My intent is not to create a technical resource for scholars. What you have in your hands serves an ambitious yet simple threefold purpose. My intent is for individuals within the body of Christ and those seeking after Him, to understand the impact of praying during the midnight season, what it means for each person's situation and how to apply the principles in fulfilling your God-given purpose here on earth.

"My people are destroyed for lack of knowledge".

✦— Hosea 4:6

This book is for believers of Christ, who despite faithfully serving Jesus, are plagued with life issues that defies logic— issues that are not making sense. It is for those Christians who, despite a great worship experience, are still battling internally with situations that they cannot speak publicly about.

iii

It is for those who know that there is more to the problems they face but do not know how to handle them. It is for those who are sick, who have tried the best medical care, yet whose condition baffles physicians. It is for that married couple who is enjoying marital bliss and shortly after marriage one spouse is mysteriously seriously injured or suffers one miscarriage after another despite no medical explanation. It is for those whose life is at a standstill despite everything they tried. It is for that family that was known for their happy home but somehow, without reasonable cause, it strangely scattered. It is for that promising child who excelled but who strangely is unable to pass that all-important exam or who is suddenly plagued with the spirit of madness. It is for that individual who is constantly dealing with recurring promises and failures, be it in marriage, destiny helpers, or favour. It is for that employee who works hard, is due to be promoted, but mysteriously falls ill and is unable to occupy that admirable position. It is for those individuals who were once successful but are somehow strangely barely making it, it is for those whose life is reflective of those who are marching on the same spot and going around in circles. Since God is love, it is uncharacteristic of Him to give blessing and add sorrow. (Proverbs 10:22).

The nameless unseen woman quietly crept up behind Jesus and touched the hem of his garment and her faith brought healing. Interestingly, nobody in that large crowd cared about that woman, nobody saw her, she was unimportant. Even though she was in the crowd with the disciples, she was not a part of the crowd. She was simply heading in another direction. So too, this book is for that wife, that mother, that father, that

iv

son, that daughter, that worshipper who is crying out "I am not insane; things are happening. The occurrences and patterns in my life are not making sense. Please help me now!".

This book is written from experiential knowledge, out of love, and with love. It is very possible that as you absorb the contents in this book you will get angry. That in itself is not bad as you will get angry for the right reasons. Who will you be angry at? The devil, the enemy of God, the adversary of our soul. You will get angry in your spirit as you unearth that the enemy without just cause has swooped into your life resulting in the dismal situations you are currently in. It will push you to a place of enough is enough. It is this anger that will prompt you into strategic, intensified prayer. Yes! repeated negativity is a symptom of captivity. It is to remind all that the power of Jesus Christ is always available to heal, deliver and set free.

As you read this book, I pray that God, through the empowering of His Holy Spirit, will help you learn, understand and apply what His Word says. May you embrace the meaning of what is contained here and understand its relevance to your situation. This book is steeped in the Good News that Jesus has never lost a battle with the devil. To be victorious, the enemy must be challenged with the Word of God, who has enabled us with the necessary power to wield against and trample upon serpents and scorpions, knowing that absolutely nothing shall in any means harm us. (Luke 10:19). The information contained therein is life-changing!

INTRODUCTION

To be successful in life, it is critical for us to understand the true purpose for our existence on this earth. To do so, each individual needs to realize that life is spiritual. The answer to this bold statement is located in Genesis 1:1. In the beginning, God *created* the earth. He did not invent it. Though there are sociological and scientific aspects to our lives, our existence here on earth is much more spiritual. There are two realms: the spiritual and the natural. The spiritual is more impactful and superimposes itself on the natural. In other words, events occur in the spiritual before manifesting in the natural. The birth of Jesus Christ was spiritual. As humans, we are spirit beings. The follower of Christ who understands this reality is therefore far advanced in his spiritual walk than the one who does not.

This book explains the intensity of midnight—both in the kingdom of darkness and the mystery of midnight prayer—

and how victory was achieved through it. Having gained this understanding, you will never again baffle over situations that do not make sense or are not adding up in the natural realm. In the spiritual realm, one plus one does not always equal two.

Furthermore, this book encourages you to embrace the power of spiritual discernment, empowering you to walk in alignment with the spirit and navigate life's challenges with newfound clarity and confidence. By understanding the profound interplay between the spiritual and natural realms, you will be equipped to fulfill your God-given purpose and experience victory in every aspect of life.

CHAPTER 1

THE POWER OF
MIDNIGHT PRAYER

nderstanding the spirituality of life is the first mystery. If life is spiritual, it means our living is spiritual, and hence it is unwise not to factor this reality into the realms of the spirit as we live our lives on this earth. As we spend time in the Word of God, we are afforded the opportunity to be able to sense the impulses of the Spirit, which is twofold:

+ To know the speakings of God.

+ To understand the movement of the Creator.

The Bible refers to this as discernment, which is the capacity to function in the impulses of the spirit.

Life and everything around us, including the earth upon which we walk, are spiritual. You and I, as entities, are spiritual. Comprehending this is one of the keys to spiritual intelligence, which every believer must possess.

It is baffling that only the wicked—agents of the devil, destiny destroyers, witches, and wizards—**seem to understand this reality to its fullest extent.**

On the contrary, the average believer is often aware of the general nature of life but lacks a complete understanding that one of the main keys to spiritual intelligence is recognizing that life, in all its aspects, is spiritual, no matter how trivial it may seem. This understanding enables us to **see the line connecting the dots.**

One of the most important weapons that must be deployed at the midnight hour is prayer, which is both communion with God and confrontation with the enemy. Prayer is wrestling; it is a ladder that we climb on to access the throne of God. Nothing comes to us easily. It means we have to understand spiritual legislation and know how to fight in the spirit in order to live a victorious life. As believers, we are Christian soldiers. A soldier who is not armoured is almost sure to become a casualty. The same holds true for those who do not invest time in spiritual things. The result is unfulfilled lives.

"But the natural man receiveth not the things of the Spirit of God, for they are foolishness unto him; neither can he know them, because they are spiritually discerned."

— 2 Corinthians 2:14

"At midnight I will rise to give thanks unto thee because of thy righteous judgments."

— Psalm 119:62

During this specific time, many unusual spiritual activities occur—activities from God and from Satan. There are two forces in this world: the Kingdom of God and the kingdom of darkness, controlled by the adversary of our souls, Satan. When we are sleeping, we are very vulnerable because we are in an unconscious state. Satan and his demons are very active during this time; their sole purpose is to thwart and destroy the lives and destiny of believers.

Believers, from time to time, comfort themselves by saying, I did no wrong; I mind my own business. So why would anyone want to interfere with me? The devil, Satan, is the great enemy of both God and humanity. As long as you have surrendered to Christ, you are an enemy of Satan. The enemy attacks God's followers by using his agents. Satan has many agents under his control. He engages men and women as agents to promote sin and make it attractive. He is very successful in his plans of deception because he transforms himself through his agents into angels of light. He is very successful in using those who profess to be Christians for his demonic work. This is because the more influential these professed Christians are, and the more knowledge they claim to have of God, the more useful they become to the Kingdom of darkness. Their assignment is to wreak havoc in the lives of believers. One of the keys to spiritual intelligence is to come to terms with life and everything about it, no matter how trivial it seems.

"They do not sleep until they do evil, and their sleep flees away until they fulfil their desires."

✦ Proverbs 4:16

One sinner disguised as an angel of light can do incalculable harm. Believers are especially susceptible to attacks because of **bloodline traits**. There is a relationship between life and blood. Satan operates on technicality. Many of the attacks facing believers today are foundational in nature.

"When the foundations are being destroyed, what can the righteous do?"

╋━━ Psalm 11:3

The enemy stands on this technicality to attack believers. It is true that no one chose their lineage. Many of our ancestors, through ignorance, legitimately entered into covenants and contracts with the enemy because they were seeking help from spirits. This was despite knowing that a body without spirit is dead. (James 2:26). They were deceived by the great deceiver, Satan, who acted like God. Believers should cancel this accusation by invoking the blood of Jesus shed on Calvary's cross as payment for our sins against the accuser. It is against this background that Daniel, the great intercessor, prayed

"We have sinned and done wrong. We have been wicked and have rebelled; we have turned away from your commands and laws."

╋━━ Daniel 9:5

In 2 Kings 6:13-14, when the King of Syria sought to arrest Elisha, he did not come by day; he came by night. As far as the kingdom of darkness is concerned, the night is their meeting time. It is their conference time, their hour to gather and deliver reports. They deliberate, strategize, and create evil plans, deciding whom to destroy and whom to leave. It is their chief planning time to destroy destinies, including those of Christians. This is when they renew evil covenants and reinforce their wicked altars. It is also the time they oversee the burdens and punishments they impose on others.

What is Midnight Prayer?

It is prayer offered to God within a time range from 12:00 midnight until 3:00 a.m., at any point within this time range. The word "midnight" is recorded fourteen times in the Bible and is always associated with some demonstration of the power of God—either in salvation or in judgment. Hence, midnight serves as a pivotal hour marking transition, judgment, and divine intervention. Midnight is a transitional time, a time when destinies are shifted in the realms of the spirit. Jesus puts it this way:

> "And while the men are sleeping, his enemy came and sowed weeds in the midst of the wheat and went away."

+—— Matthew 13:25

This illustration by Jesus has many spiritual lessons. The only reason the enemy successfully planted evil seeds on the same farm was because the watchmen were not keeping guard. Understanding the spiritual legislation gives you understanding over others. Grasping this understanding means that you as an individual will value prayer knowing that when we pray among many other things we are shifting things in the realms of the spirit which means we will never try to fight our battles in the physical.

Midnight is the hour of asking, seeking, and knocking on doors. It is the time to petition Heaven. At this hour, things begin to happen. No wonder the Word of God says,

"This book of the law shall not depart out of your mouth, but you shall meditate upon it day and night."

Joshua 1:8

Midnight is the time to meditate on the Word of God, to locate relevant Scripture, and to reflect on them. This period of midnight between 12:00 and 3:00 a.m. is a vulnerable time in the realm of the bondwoman, as they do not pray at that time. The best time to catch a thief is when the thief is in the act.

'Lest Satan should take advantage of us; for we are not ignorant of his devices."

2 Cor. 2: 11

The kingdom of darkness is extremely active during the midnight hours—the period between 12:00 a.m. and 3:00 a.m. This is the most active time in the spiritual world. Darkness is when all that is evil and wicked is let loose upon the earth. The Bible talks about the midnight cry, signaling the greatest time of struggle between good and evil, or a time of great controversy. If we are not petitioning the throne of God at midnight, the devil is busy unleashing havoc in the lives of believers. We are either aligned for life or for death! During this active time, there are often visitations—whether demonic or angelic. We must understand that those who control the night infiltrate the day.

From a biblical perspective, the midnight period not only represents a literal time but also signifies deep transitions showcasing God's intervention, especially during times of crisis, judgment, and miracles. It is one of the most important and powerful times to engage in prayer since it is the time of night when the enemy gathers to destroy the destinies of believers. This crucial time is, therefore, a time of battle between good and evil, between the believer and the devil. During this time, many evil activities like movement and flying are operational.

Knowing how devastating fear is, the Bible records "Do not be afraid" three hundred and sixty-five times.

"Thou shalt not be afraid of the terror by night nor the arrows that fly by day."

✦ Psalms 91:5

The first mention of the word midnight in scripture is in the book of Exodus and was enacted by God Himself as He launched the final attack on Egypt. The Lord said, "About midnight will I go out into the midst of Egypt: and all the firstborn in the land of Egypt shall die, from the firstborn of Pharaoh that sits upon his throne, even unto the firstborn of the maidservant that is behind the mill; and all the firstborn of beasts" (Exodus 11:4-5). This attack led to the instantaneous release of the Israelites from the land of bondage. Notice, it was done at the midnight battlegate with a resounding victory.

Jesus Christ created each human with beautiful destinies, meaning that each human has a purpose here on this earth. Everything God created, the enemy comes up with a counterfeit. The sole purpose of the adversary, the enemy of our souls, is to destroy the destiny of believers—to prevent and block that which God intended for our lives, to prevent believers from coming into their greatness.

"The thief comes only to steal and kill and destroy; I have come that they may have life, and have it to the full".

— John 10:10

The best time for the kingdom of darkness to launch this attack is during the midnight hour, a crucial time in the realms of the spirit. Midnight (between 12:00 a.m. and 3:00 a.m.) is the most spiritually active period of the day. During this time, attacks, dreams, revelations, and visitations from the spirit world—both angelic and demonic—often occur, especially when we are sleeping. This is the time when we are most vulnerable. One's life and destiny can be decided during this time. In other words, battles are taking place.

The impact of midnight prayers is crucial to the lives of believers who understand the mystery surrounding this spiritual exercise. It is extremely difficult for Christians to overcome and obtain total breakthrough without praying during this crucial time at night. Midnight is either the preceding day or the following day. This period is extremely powerful, the most spiritually active period of the day, and it is therefore wise to engage in it spiritually. Midnight is a strategic time for prayer. If the day is coming, we are at midnight—this allows us to speak into the next day for our favour. It is a time of transition.

At this crucial time, the destinies of men are shaped and interrupted. Strategically, Satan launches attacks at midnight. For example, the enemy often feeds people in their dreams; others are raped, robbed, injected, or even fall sick, even though they went to bed healthy.

Since it is a very active time in the spirit world, it should never be taken for granted, since, from experiential knowledge, one's destiny can be exchanged. The enemy is very comfortable using midnight to cause trouble—this is his ultimate purpose. There are battles at midnight. This is evident in the familiar story of the woman who snuffed out the life of her child and then exchanged her dead child for the living baby. The evil exchange happened during the crucial time of midnight (1 Kings 3:20). The midnight period is a moment of defining destiny. Through no fault of others, this woman used her own hands to destroy her destiny. She was unable to care for her own child, resulting in his death. How, then, would she be able to take care of what is not hers?

The aim of the enemy is to steal, kill, and destroy. Many evil exchanges occur because people have used their own hands to circumvent and destroy their own destinies, resulting in covetousness for someone else's.

The destiny that was rightfully theirs was either not properly taken care of or was carelessly handled, leading to its destruction. This carelessness on the mother's part caused the death of her child. Sadly, this mother used her own body to slay her own child, reducing her to childlessness and placing her in the same state she was in prior to being blessed with the fruit of the womb, hence the reason she wanted to steal the blessings of the other mother. This is how destinies are switched in the realms of the spirit. She waited until midnight because she knew that the mother of the other baby would be in deep sleep. Who switched your colourful destiny? Who has taken your life of peace and has replaced it with a life of turmoil? Who took your life of comfort and replaced it with impoverishment, struggle and hardship? But thank God, the same midnight was the time for slaying—the angel of God came and slew 185,000 powers of the enemy.

During this crucial time at night, satanic worshippers and agents of the devil are at their best, busily polluting the lives of believers, making every attempt to disrupt the promises of God for them. They devise plans against the counsel of God concerning one's life.

Another parable He put forth to them, saying:

"The kingdom of heaven is like a man who sowed good seed in his field; but while men slept, his enemy came and sowed tares among the wheat and went his way."

✦—— Matthew 13:24-43

Spiritually speaking, any Christian who is not watchful and

vigilant, nor a doer of midnight prayers, will give the enemy an opportunity to plant all manner of troubles in that individual's life. This explains why there are many faithful Christians whose lives are full of problems—stagnation, setbacks, and unexplained delays, seeing the blessing but being unable to touch it, getting so near yet so far. The reason for this is that they are fast asleep when they should be alert and praying.

One way to know that the enemy is on the prowl is when sleep is interrupted unnecessarily in the night. This could be the Holy Spirit nudging you to pray. It could very well be the time the enemy is plotting your demise.

Praying at midnight is highly spiritual and highly strategic in warfare. Matthew 13:25 reminds us that while men slept, his enemies came and sowed tares among the wheat and went his way. The hours between 12:00 midnight and 3:00 a.m. are when a high traffic of business is transacted in the spirit realm. Your success or failure can be decided during this time. So, if you have serious business to transact in the spirit realm, these hours are the best time. As you read your Bible, you will find many midnight deliverances. If you effectively utilize this prayer period, you will also experience breakthroughs.

"Jesus Christ is the same yesterday, today, and forever."

+—— Hebrews 13:8

We have to understand that many things happen to people at night when it is dark. The destinies of people are exchanged by night. During this time, evil forces play with the destiny of men like a chess game. This is the time the kingdom of darkness gathers to devise against the will of God for believers. The Bible describes it as "terror by night," not just terrorism as we know it. Life is spiritual! "Thou shalt not be afraid of the arrows that fly by day." Have we ever seen the arrows that are flying? We get up and leave our homes with the intention to return, and then something happens. An arrow is that which wounds, harms a person physically, emotionally, relationally, financially, spiritually, these arrows from the kingdom of darkness, launches unrelenting catastrophes during the day. These arrows are invisible and are projected at targeted or untargeted persons. Life is spiritual!

What better books to teach us spiritual intelligence than the Books of Psalm, especially 91, and the Book of Job. In chapter 1, a meeting was being held in the heavenlies. Satan now comes, and a conversation is engaged. "Have you considered my servant Job?" While they are discussing this scenario, Job is on earth minding his business, and suddenly things start to nosedive in his life.

It is amazing how many people try to ignore the spirituality of life and expect to rise to the top. It is impossible. There are many things called sicknesses, and we do not even know from whence they came. Often, doctors do not know the answers simply because they are trained in natural medicine, and spiritual things cannot be cured with medicine as spiritual things are spiritually discerned.

"But the natural man receiveth not the things of the Spirit of God: for they are foolishness unto him: neither can he know them, because they are spiritually discerned".

— 1 Corinthians 2; 14-16

12

Mysteries that cannot be explained! Life is spiritual!

The key to survival is to become spiritually minded. There are mysteries in people's families that they do not understand. A lot of these secrets are located in one's foundation. Revelation surrounding these mysteries, and how to be set free from them are birthed during prayer at the midnight season.

When Jesus came, His birth was spiritual. Consequently, in the realms of the spirit, we do not have to tell anyone our names. We are already identified by bloodline.

"When the foundations are destroyed, what can the righteous do?"

✦——— Psalm 11:3

The midnight period is when the powers of darkness gather to make decisions and carry out their villainous acts against their victims—those who have chosen Christ. The Bible mentions the "terror by night" and "pestilence that walks in darkness" in Psalm 91. Hence, Christians are encouraged to make use of this time in prayer and will undoubtedly have a spiritual advantage over those who do not. Samson was in the Philistines camp because he was chasing a woman. The Philistines were determined to kill Samson since he was a thorn in their flesh. He was a warrior, they were unable to figure him out. The enemy can sense one's greatness. The enemy will always go after those who are anointed, those who can make an impact, those that will influence the world and community for Jesus Christ. He is after the oil that is upon their lives, simply because they are threats to his kingdom. When the enemy is after you, he is not only coming to attack or steal, his ultimate aim is to kill you. Samson, recognizing the midnight strategy, lay until midnight to spring a dangerous surprise on his enemies. Samson recognized that worrying would not help. If he made any movement the enemies would be alerted and he would be overpowered.

Samson exercised spiritual intelligence by waiting for the time of the spirit. At midnight he caught up with the time of the spirit, the time of encounters and heavy angelic traffic. Even though the gates are unbreakable, Samson took hold of the gates and carried them to the top of a hill on his shoulder. He recognized that at midnight the power of his strength would be activated. Like Samson, you can strategize and overturn every demonic trap planned against your destiny by making use of the midnight season thus fulfilling what is written of you in the volumes of the Book.

"And Samson lay till midnight, and arose at midnight, and took the doors of the gate of the city, and the two posts, and went away with them, bar and all, and put them upon his shoulders, and carried them up to the top of a hill that is before Hebron."

Judges 16:3

The Psalmist David in Psalm 91 describes a secret place. Needless to say, this is a very familiar Psalm. In other words, David was making reference to an address for those who need safety. He stated that those who are fortunate enough to find such an address will as a result abide under the shadow of the Almighty. This statement implies that "shadow" has a spiritual implication. Although physics states that when light is cast on an object it creates a shadow, the Bible tells us that men can dwell under God's shadow. David sought to explain this in a three-dimensional way:

+ Man coming under the shadow
+ God as our refuge and fortress
+ God—us trusting in Him

It is important to note that although we do not see these descriptions through an optical lens, the effects are nevertheless physical, again reinforcing that life is spiritual.

"He will deliver thee from the fowler and from the noisome pestilence." The Psalmist is describing strange things unable to be seen with our natural eyes. However, the effects are physical. The description continues, "He shall cover thee with His feathers. His truth shall be our shield and buckler," indicating that truth is objective, it is a reality and is relatable. A further description is given in verse 5, referred to as "terror by night." The Bible is letting us know that once there is night, there is what is called "terror by night," irrespective of how peaceful an environment may seem (Psalm 91:3-5).

During the time of sleep, of time of vulnerability, that is the time you are pruned to attacks from the kingdom of darkness. Attacks such as being suffocated, being held down, being fed in the dream, being stripped naked, shaving of the head. It is during this time that the enemy sows disappointment, shame, setback, rejection and places spiritual embargo against one's career and destiny. During this time is when one's destiny and advancement is caged. During this time that an individual's hands and feet are satanically shackled. It is during this time that the demonic limitations and restrictions are placed to cage one's destiny. The battle rages for the fulfilment of our destinies during the midnight hour. No wonder we are forewarned that we wrestle, meaning our fight is not against flesh and blood; we are fighting dark forces, spirits without bodies that function like you and I. We wrestle against principalities and powers. The rulers of darkness cannot function or rule in the light. The moment there is physical darkness, the rulers of the night are thereby authorized to appear in the description the Bible calls "terror by night." There are levels of spiritual heights that one cannot attain without mastering the art of praying at midnight. So too, there is no telling how far we can go spiritually when we engage in praying at certain strategic hours in the night.

How can you overcome your enemies without praying at the midnight hour?

Activities from God

Most humans sleep during this time, which means the body is often weaker. This weakness, therefore, makes us vulnerable to spiritual attacks or satanic manipulations (Matthew 13:25), making it a good time for the enemy and his agents to launch their attack.

One of the most powerful spiritual tools that God has given, but is vastly ignored in Christendom, is the midnight prayer strategy. There is something about night prayers that is so powerful, and the enemy knows this. He is very much aware! He is very upset when believers gather to pray at the midnight hour because it paralyzes his plans. Devil worshippers, witches, and Satanists have discovered this secret and are using it on a daily basis to destroy lives.

From the Bible and through the ages, the prayers done around this particular time have always brought tremendous and unprecedented results.

CHAPTER 2

THE MIDNIGHT STRATEGY

It is through the study of God's word that we discover the truth. There are many biblical examples of those who fought and won during the midnight period. Our first example has always been Jesus Christ of Nazareth, the greatest exemplar. David, a man despite his failures, whom God nonetheless described as "one after His own heart," never lost a single battle. Why? At midnight, he gave praises to God. Great nations were destroyed because their armies were sleeping at midnight. God waited until midnight to execute judgment on the Egyptians since it was a time of vulnerability.

When the Israelites were in Egyptian captivity, it was at midnight that God chose to destroy the Egyptians while they worshipped at the River Nile. Witches and wizards also cast their spells at midnight, worshipped their gods, and invoked marine spirits from the River Nile. The all-knowing God chose this time to defile their powers. At this strategic time, the battle, as instructed by God to Moses, would be between the King of Kings and the gods of Egypt—the powers of the satanic world vs. the Superior Power. Exodus 11:4 states, "Then Moses said, 'Thus says the Lord: About midnight, I will go out into the midst of Egypt.'" During this divine visitation, all the firstborn of the Egyptians, both human and animal, were destroyed by God.

Using this opportune time, **at midnight**, the Lord struck down all the firstborn in Egypt, from the firstborn of Pharaoh, who sat on the throne, to the firstborn of the prisoner in the dungeon, and the firstborn of all the livestock. Pharaoh and all his officials and all the Egyptians got up during the night, and there was loud wailing in Egypt, for there was not a house without someone dead (Exodus 12:29-30). Stubborn Pharaoh was adamant that he would not let the Israelite children go despite the pleadings of Moses. However when God showed up at midnight and released his judgement on the Egyptians, he called Moses and begged him to let them go. Until we confront that deity, that evil altar from which the kingdom of darkness reigns, we will not come into that which God has destined for us.

As has been shown, it is at midnight that the enemy often programs the failure of men.

I have come to realize that Satan is strategic in his plans to tempt and harass mankind, specifically those who have chosen to follow Jesus as their Lord. Day and night, we are terrorized by his and his demons' influence. The Bible says to "Keep your senses, be watchful. Your adversary, the Devil, walks about like a roaring lion, seeking to devour someone" (1 Peter 5:8).

In the heavenly court of God, Jehovah asked Satan a question, and the response he gave is recorded in (Job 2:1–5).

Eliphaz, Job's friend, was visited during the night (Job 4:12–21). Knowing that Satan is dedicated to our destruction, God has given us protections. He teaches us about his adversary so that we are not in the dark (2 Cor 2:11). We are instructed to put on the whole armour of God (Eph 6:11–16). When we wear this armour and resist the Devil, he will flee (James 4:7). That is why it is important that we do as the scriptures counsel (Eph 4:27). Throughout the day and night, I remain vigilant, never laying down the suit of armour.

As followers of Christ, it is critical that we live a life of intentional vigilance. There are heights that cannot be attained in the spirit realm without mastering the art of praying at midnight. Any unjust situation can be overturned at the midnight hour. Throughout biblical times and through the ages, midnight prayers have brought tremendous and unprecedented results. During this time, believers should be busy speaking their destinies into being—speaking their prophecy, their glory, and all that God has said to them into being. As demonstrated by Jesus, it is during this time that occultic powers are confronted with prayers and decrees. Since the dark world speaks and makes declarations of failure and doom, prayers and declarations simply counteract their efforts.

There are levels of revelation that will not be revealed without prolonged midnight prayers. Upon surrendering one's life to Christ, we are like newborn babies, relying on others to pray for us and carry us in our faith for a time. However, after a while, we are expected to start growing, walking, and using our own authority. There are also demonic strongholds, chains, thrones, generational curses, and entities that will never be dismantled unless through intentional, prolonged midnight battles.

The aim of this book is to alert Christians once again to this great spiritual weapon that God Himself has made available to us. I believe, and through experience too, that any Christian who masters the art of praying in the midnight season will ultimately control what happens during their day. Those who do not strategize in this kingdom are the ones who lose.

The disciples were fishing all night, yet they caught nothing. Jesus' instruction to them was clear, intentional, and divine: "Cast it on the other side!" At no time did Jesus instruct them to change the river. It was the same water, the same net with no holes, and the same men. They had everything right; however, something prevented their harvest from manifesting. Despite their experience as fishermen, they were stuck in spiritual mediocrity. Midnight prayers will equip believers with the necessary depth to overcome the adversary.

There is no way to confront an enemy that has reinforced itself with a mere pat on the back. Midnight prayer gives us that extra edge to defeat an enemy who has a track record of resurfacing and putting on new appearances from time to time. Midnight prayer is one of those weapons that announce your destination. Targeted prayer spreads casualties throughout the enemy's camp.

Notwithstanding, it is a great time for deliverance (Acts 16:25). It has the highest potency for getting answers to prayers.

It helps in crucifying the flesh, builds spiritual discipline, and enhances spiritual stamina. During this crucial hour, when the enemy and his demonic hosts are busy subverting the destiny of men, those who are praying block the projections, the evil speaking, pronouncements, and attacks that are being launched. The prayers offered during this time cancel what the kingdom of darkness is unleashing, nullifying its manipulations. Many Christians today are not spiritually alert, nor do they place great value on midnight prayers. As a result, the devil capitalizes on this error and sows numerous problems in their lives. There are many believers faithfully serving God, yet they face obstacles and setbacks that could have been averted had they made use of this sacrificial time of prayer.

Ruth 3:8 states,
"And it came to pass at midnight that a man was afraid, and turned himself in, and a woman lay at his feet."

Ruth discovered her husband at midnight. Here we see that midnight is the best time to pray for marriage. Are you seeking a spouse? Midnight is the best time to pray for God to give you a godly wife or husband.

In conclusion, the midnight hour is a strategic time for spiritual warfare and personal breakthroughs. Whether seeking divine intervention, protection, or blessings, midnight prayers give believers a unique spiritual advantage. As illustrated through various biblical examples, there is unparalleled power in midnight prayer. Those who embrace this practice will experience profound changes in their lives and the manifestation of God's will. Let us be intentional, steadfast, and spiritually alert, knowing that the midnight hour is not just a time of rest, but a time of battle and victory.

CHAPTER 3

THE MYSTERY OF DARKNESS AND SPIRITUAL WARFARE

Darkness has divisive powers—it separates. We must understand the mystery of spiritual legislation: the ability to invoke spiritual realities and bring our lives into obedience to Christ. We must learn how to pray until victory is achieved, keeping in mind that we do not pray until we are tired—we pray until peace is reached. Sometimes peace will come quickly, other times it will arrive after two days, three weeks, months, or longer. We must trust God for the grace to endure. In other words, we must "stick it out."

Notice that at times, in the wee hours of the morning, you should be sleeping, but as you turn in your bed, you realize that the atmosphere is not sanitized. What is the next step? You simply turn to one side, open your mouth, and declare, "Let God arise, let my enemies be scattered." You turn to the other side, repeating the declaration, stretching while doing so, and saying, "Lord, fight for me. Plead my cause, O God.".

In essence, you are letting the territory know that **a king or queen who is asleep is still a king or queen.** In darkness, your best friend could betray you without your knowledge. By now, we understand that darkness is more conducive to satanic operations. So, when Christians tarry in prayer during the night, they are suspending all astral travel and throwing spiritual stones, spanners, and hammers at the work of the enemy. That is why midnight is the best time to instill fear into your enemy through their own dreams and visions. When your enemies are sleeping, you can pray prayers that will thwart their plans and throw them into disarray. **This is the mystery of the night.**

Our world is not solely scientific; the spiritual realm is more powerful than the natural realm. The spiritual realm superimposes itself on the natural realm. The adversary, Satan, is a manipulator. The first thing he manipulated with our first parents, Adam and Eve—especially Eve—was their sight. The issue started when she saw. She simply acted upon what she saw:

"And when the woman saw that the tree was good for food, and that it was pleasant to the eyes, and a tree to be desired to make one wise, she took of the fruit thereof, and did eat, and gave also unto her husband with her; and he did eat."

— Genesis 3:6, KJV

The fall in the Garden of Eden occurred because the power of Adam and Eve's sight was manipulated. The enemy cast an image upon them, and they responded to it.

One will agree that while we can doubt what we hear, it is difficult to doubt what we see. One's success in life is therefore predicated on their ability to see. The privilege of the seeing eye is critical for one's success. It was through a dream that the Lord spoke to Abimelech. He intended to take Abraham's wife when he was warned that this was a covenant woman with a covenant child. In the morning, he arose, gave Abraham gifts, and left Egypt wealthy as a result. The greatest danger any human being faces in the spiritual realm is what happens when that individual is asleep.

Agents of the devil typically operate by launching their attacks while their victims are asleep, that is, unconscious. The enemy knows that when men are sleeping, they are in an unconscious state. This explains why most attacks happen during this time. By the time they wake up, they often find everything going wrong, with situations that defy logic and reason. Life is spiritual. The kingdom of darkness attacks businesses, ministries, churches, men and women of God, marriages, relationships, health, and more. Sometimes, the destinies of victims are taken to the enemy's meeting places, or covens (a group of witches who meet frequently), where they are tied up or even destroyed. God knew how terrible these wicked agents of Satan are when he commanded Israel not to allow them to remain alive (Deuteronomy 20:16-18).

How to Overcome

✦

To battle and defeat these agents of darkness, who mostly operate at midnight, you must also wake up at this time to pray. In other words, you must release the fire of God against the fire from the kingdom of darkness. You must wake up and render their evil arrows, enchantments, curses, and chants against your life and that of your loved ones impotent. Not only that, but you can also cause serious and perpetual havoc in their covens. All this is only possible through powerful and sustained scripture-based midnight prayers.

The body of Christ must immediately awaken to the great power that God has graciously placed in our hands. Midnight signifies a time of adversity, but also a time of undying faith and divine intervention leading to freedom and salvation for those who are spiritually alert. If you seek to step into your God-given assignment, you must strategize to win. You can shift the destiny of your children during the midnight season. God has given us authority.

Perhaps you are having an interview in the morning for that job you applied for. Use the midnight to claim ownership of that position by placing a demand on that company that they are unable to hire anyone else. Going into that interview, you have confidence knowing that you have denied everyone else. Therefore, it is unscriptural for the agents of darkness to prevail against believers when we have been given the authority to trample on serpents and scorpions and over all— not some—of the power of the enemy (Luke 10:19). Midnight prayers bring about midnight victors.

Do you want to offer the kind of praise to God that will cause the heavens to shake? Do you want God to intervene in your situation? Use the midnight season for praise and worship. This is evidenced in Psalm 119:62: "At midnight I will rise to give thanks unto thee because of thy righteous judgments." By doing so, you cannot lose a single battle. Try it and see! When you are finished, start dancing over your situation. In Judges 16:3, we see that Samson arose at midnight, took the doors of the city gate, and carried them to the top of a hill before Hebron. Christians need to follow Samson's example.

Spiritually alert Christians do not sleep too much at midnight. Real Christian soldiers recognize the importance of midnight prayers. Even if they sleep at times, they remain conscious in the spirit. The devil will not mess with such a person because they are spiritually alert. The truth is, the Christians who are spiritually effective, the ones with numerous testimonies, are those who convert their night seasons into midnight prayers. These individuals have an upper hand in the fight of faith and are not easily defeated by the adversary. No wonder David, an effective prayer warrior and strategist, declared in Psalm 119:62:

"At midnight I will rise to give thanks unto thee because of thy righteous judgments."

CHAPTER 4

THE SACRIFICE OF PRAISE

God rewards sacrifice. Believers should know that there are controlling powers that continue to see that negative prophecies are enforced in the lives of God's children. Until the Saints of God understand how to legislate by the spirit, we will continue to be victims of men. One of the ways that we engage the wisdom of God is when we pray at strategic times. Great men contact power when men sleep. If anyone is afflicted, the remedy for such individuals is to pray–not to grumble, complain or express self pity, which enables the kingdom of darkness–but to pray. In other words, the remedy for any affliction is prayer (James 5:13). Prayer is a very powerful weapon in all seasons of one's life, but especially in the midnight season.

Any unjust situation against one's life and family can be overturned at the midnight hour by engaging in strategic, Scripture-based prayer and praise. This was evidenced by Paul and Silas, two prayer intercessors in the Bible. Perhaps there are situations in your life that seem to have no answer. Decrees and declarations at midnight can be very effective. If your business is not going well, a targeted prayer for this situation would be: "Let the spiritual gates over my business be opened in the name of Jesus." Do you need church growth? The same holds true. Praying for the grace that delivered Paul and Silas can be your portion. Jesus said, "I have come that you might have life and have it more abundantly."

Paul and Silas demonstrated great faith because they not only knew of God, but had a relationship with Him. They understood that when praises go up, blessings come down, as the Bible admonishes. It was at midnight that they were singing hymns to God while the other prisoners listened. Suddenly, a great earthquake occurred, shaking the foundations of the prison. Why were these two prayer warriors praying at night? Night indicates darkness, the absence of light. Night begins at sunset and is widely considered unsuitable for labour. Jesus said,

"I must work the works of Him who sent me while it is day;
the night is coming when no one can work"

✦— John 9:4

We must demonstrate true faith, which enables us to pray with power and achieve results. Faith cannot be reasoned with; attempting to do so equates God to man. Faith is one of the main accompaniments to prayer. Those in the world operate by saying, Show me, and I will go. For the believer, it's, I do not see it yet, but I know by faith it is coming.

"Let not your faith weaken, for the blessings received are proportionate to the faith exercised." (Acts of the Apostles, page 521)Those who come to Christ must believe that He exists. As citizens of the kingdom of God, we operate on the premise of faith. The disciples lacked mustard-seed faith, and to correct this, they needed to engage in prayer and fasting for themselves. The Bible says that without faith, it is impossible to please Him (Hebrews 11:6).

Night is designed for rest and it is favourable for the purpose of the wicked. It is the most active period of time in the spirit realm. Your life, your rise or fall can be decided during this time, the battle of the night. It is no wonder the Shepherds of the Bible were watching their flocks by night because they were cognizant of the dangerous thieves and animals that roam about at night. It is because of the **absence of light** that the night is so dangerous and is a period of severe calamities. Darkness causes people to wander aimlessly, believing they are safe when danger lurks. It is in the darkness that people stumble. Paul and Silas understood the mystery of midnight prayer; hence, they were singing and praying. They sang and prayed, when morning arrived, victory was already achieved. Wow! **The mystery of midnight prayer.**

If you are conscious of praying at midnight, you will know that the night is a period of aggressive response from heaven. In the Book of Acts (Acts 16:25), these two prayer intercessors, though in jail, waited until midnight before starting any activity. At midnight, they began singing praises to God and were delivered. They had been in prison all day, but they waited until midnight. There was a reason for that—

strategy! They invested in their destiny by using the instrumentality of prayer at a strategic time. Men of fire are men of power. Paul and Silas shifted their destiny by engaging in praise and prayer, which released mayhem in the camp of their conspirators and birthed their freedom. Christians are followers of Christ. Jesus often prayed at night, setting an example. How about His followers?

Of course, it requires great sacrifice for a Christian to burn the midnight oil, waking up at midnight to pray, especially when stubborn situations refuse to bow. The enemy will not make it easy, knowing the victory that can be gained. One of the weapons he successfully uses against believers is the spirit of slumber. Many will effortlessly stay awake for all other activities during this time but will struggle to pray. This, in itself, is an attack! Prayer terrifies and pushes the kingdom of darkness back and the enemy is aware of this. The enemy delights when weak believers refuse to engage in prayer at this time. The key to that stubborn situation, that stronghold, that evil family pattern lies in your hands—it is a life of consistent midnight prayer. Jesus instructed,

"Arise, cry out in the night: in the beginning of the watches pour out thine heart like water before the face of the Lord: lift up thy hands toward him for the life of thy young children, that faint for hunger in the top of every street"

✦——— Lamentations 2: 19

Am I saying you have to pray from 12 a.m. to 3 a.m.? Start with small steps—even if it is 15 minutes at this critical time.

That marriage situation, that financial problem, that issue causing you to cry yourself to sleep or grow grey hairs—start praying for 15 minutes, then add more time each night. Before long, you will be praying for an hour without realizing it. The Holy Spirit will begin to quicken your spirit. It is a war between flesh and spirit. Your flesh is giving in, but your spirit knows it needs to do this. Sacrifice! Dancing is a strange mystery of deliverance. Believe what I am telling you!

There is a time to pray and a time to engage in other things. The Bible calls it the **sacrifice of praise.** It does not say "music." It is a sacrifice, but I guarantee you, it will tear your heavens open. Want to see breakthroughs? Believers should learn to rejoice before the Lord. **Nothing paralyzes Satan like the sacrifice and mystery of praise and joy.** This is another mystery of midnight prayer.

"Let them praise His name with dancing and make music to Him with timbrel and harp."

✦ Psalm 149:3

When we are ignorant that life is spiritual, and do not know the key, we cheat ourselves and victory will elude us. If we are reluctant to engage in these mysteries, some things will never happen in our lives.

You cannot compare the results you get from praying during the day with those from praying at midnight. **Praying during the day is good; praying at night is best.** These two prayer intercessors understood spiritual legislation and the rules of engagement, which is why they were victorious against the enemy's schemes. This does not mean that prayers during the day will not be heard. However, night prayers, especially midnight prayers, are sacrificial, and God responds faster to sacrifice.

From experience, I can attest to the power of midnight prayer warfare. Without this prayer strategy, the enemy would have had the upper hand in my life, and I would not have been here to write this book.

One night, during my customary time of worship, I found myself in conversation with my Heavenly Father, grappling with the confusion and challenges in my life. Despite my efforts to understand, clarity remained elusive. It was in that moment of seeking and questioning that I heard a clear instruction from the Holy Spirit: "Start praying at the midnight hour."

In obedience to this divine prompting, I began to dedicate this specific time to prayer. This was unfamiliar territory for me, and of course, I struggled at first. However, I gradually improved as the Holy Spirit strengthened me. What followed was a transformative experience. As I engaged in midnight prayer, I found that many of my questions were answered, and the weight of my concerns began to lift. It felt as though the darkness surrounding my understanding was illuminated by the light of God's presence. As promised in Scripture,

"He reveals deep and hidden things; he knows what is in the darkness, and light dwells with him."

Daniel 2:22

Midnight prayer became a sacred space where I could lay bare my heart, seek divine guidance, listen, and receive wisdom that transcended my earthly understanding. During these quiet hours, the Holy Spirit began to teach me the things of the Spirit. I learned to listen more intently and trust in the sovereignty of God. As a result, I was able to intercept and reverse numerous schemes orchestrated by the enemy against me.

It is at midnight that serious life problems are either addressed or tackled. God honours sacrifice. He values the effort of midnight prayers above all. Here is the reason: the all-knowing, all-seeing God sees your sacrifice and labour in midnight prayer warfare, and thus answers your prayer speedily. This effort demonstrates the value you place on your prayers. As Jesus instructed,

> "Gather to Me these consecrated people, who made a covenant with Me by sacrifice"
>
> ✦——— Psalm 50:5

This scripture is ominous. We see that the Saviour encourages all of His children to wake up at night and pray for their families, the youth, leaders, and nations. Yet many believers, through lack of knowledge, are unaware that the key to the solution to their problems is in their hands—persistent midnight prayer warfare. It continues to demolish strongholds. Think of a ball of ice, even though hardened, persistent chipping at it will eventually cause it to be crumbled.

Praying at midnight is a sacrifice that will not go unrewarded. The God who sees our desperation through the sacrifices we make will reward us. There seems to be a common thread that runs through those who neglect this prayer strategy for victory. Many complain that the nature of their jobs prevents them from praying at this time. The truth is, nothing should take precedence over God. A song says, "But how much I love Him my actions will show." Too often, God gets second-best or what is left of our time, even though we are not our own—we belong to Him.

"See what great love the Father has lavished on us, that we should be called children of God! And that is what we are!"

✦— 1 John 3:1

Lest we forget, He is the giver of all good gifts. He is the ultimate provider, able to give better jobs that will not take precedence over Him and will allow time in His presence. Making the sacrifice to pray during midnight dislodges satanic arrows hidden in the clouds, arrows that subvert your blessings. Failing to do this will result in working tirelessly without results. Job 4:20 affirms, "They are destroyed from morning to evening; they perish forever without anyone regarding it."

We have to understand that the spirit of a sleeping person is weak, harmless, and is comparable to an experience of death. The enemy knows this and he capitalizes on the weaknesses of individuals to undo them during this particular time of night. But if we understand the principles, we can wage war correctly and begin to get things to happen.

"Desire not the night when people are cut off in their place."

+—— Job 36:20

There are millions and millions of spirits moving about in darkness: witchcraft powers, marine spirits, wandering spirits, evil angels, satanic agents, occultic powers, recruitment agents for Satan, dream manipulators, spirit wives, spirit husbands, and powers from the moon that strike by night. Psalm 91:5-6 says, "Thou shalt not be afraid for the terror by night, nor for the arrow that flieth by day, nor for the pestilence that walketh in darkness." All these are forces. When you utilize your midnight hours in prayer, things begin to shift in your favour. **This is the second mystery.**

Benefits of Praying at the Midnight Hour

+

+ Midnight prayer allows us to hear warnings from God without distractions (Job 33:14-18).

+ It brings supernatural encounters with God through the Holy Spirit and warring angels (Joel 2:28).

+ It gives us the upper hand in spiritual warfare (1 Peter 5:6).

✦ It blocks the arrows that the enemy would send during the day against us. We send prayers ahead of us, commanding the morning, steering the wheel of the day to bring us favour. (Ephesians 6:6)

✦ It brings victory over stubborn challenges, as exemplified in the Book of Genesis, with Jacob's persistent all-night prayer. Midnight is the best time to pull down strongholds. It gives great boldness to face the enemy and achieve breakthroughs. It allows the believer to hear from God. (Isaiah 41:13)

✦ Midnight prayer positions you for divine encounters. Interestingly, Jacob knew this, and he had an uncommon encounter that changed him.

✦ Praying at midnight enables you to terminate the activities of the devil. Lest we forget, the kingdom of darkness plans their attacks at midnight. Praying at midnight directly intercepts their plans and scatters them before execution.

✦ During the midnight season, God gives spiritual directives concerning the stubborn situations in your life, family and destiny.

✦ Praying at the midnight season disconnects the source of the enemy's power.

✶ Generational curses, bloodline issues are broken through midnight prayer. 1 (Chronicle 4:9-10)

CHAPTER 5

THE PRACTICE OF PRAYER

Midnight **Prayer is not optional for Christians. There is an art of war.** Jesus encourages his followers to pray without ceasing, yet many believers are simply going through the motions. Not realizing tangible results, many have thrown their hands up in frustration, abandoned their faith, and all but given up on God due to lack of knowledge (Hosea 4:6). Having given up, they return to the one who caused their affliction in the first place—the devil.

"Like a dog that returns to his vomit is a fool who repeats his folly."

— Proverbs 26:11

Jesus has given us the power to bind and loose. Whatever we bind here on this earth is loosed in Heaven. Each believer has a responsibility to first bind before it can be loosed in

Heaven (Matthew 18:18).

"In a moment they shall surely die, and the people shall be troubled at midnight and pass away, and the mighty shall be taken away without hand."

✦——— Job 34:20

This means that despite the evildoers defending themselves, despite the enemies of God hiding themselves, as you apply the mystery of midnight prayers, God will set you free and destroy the stronghold of the mighty. I must reiterate that midnight is the period for you to destroy the destroyer. Believers, do not run away from people issuing threats or threatening you. Instead, gather together at midnight to deal with them. This is a strategy largely ignored in Christendom. You get up at midnight and raise an altar to God, and your altar begins to speak. Woe to any power of the night that has gathered against you at that hour.

In order to control the activities around us, and severely dismantle and dislodge satanic ordinances against us, our family, and the church, one must learn to wake up at midnight to fight with the Word of God in prayer against the powers of darkness. For example, the activities of witches and wizards. The Word of God is the bullet, prayer is the rifle.

There are agents of darkness possessed by the terrible, merciless, and destructive spirit of witchcraft. This spirit is known to be very wicked. The effect can be seen on victims, especially in the case of strange undiagnosed illnesses. This spirit delights in causing harm and, oftentimes, the total destruction of human beings. The agents of the kingdom of darkness are without mercy. The word "mercy" is not in their vocabulary, since they bear the characteristics of their father, Satan. They enjoy seeing the suffering of God's children. Agents are those who have rejected Christ and have embraced Satan, thus working with him to carry out his ills against those who have rejected him. When Satan's bewitching power sways a person, God is forgotten, and man, who is loaded with corrupt motives, is lauded. Evil is secretly practiced by these deceived souls as a virtue. This is a species of witchcraft.

"He was a murderer from the beginning, and has nothing to do with the truth, because there is no truth in him. When he lies, he speaks according to his own nature, for he is a liar and the father of lies."

— John 8:44

That is why a person, even at times family members, close friends, and associates, will for unknown reasons turn against those closest to them.

"For the son treats the father with contempt, the daughter rises up against her mother, the daughter-in-law against her mother in law; a man's enemies are the men of his own house".

— Micah 7:6

Such people, who are influenced and possess this evil spirit, can actually proceed to harm the individuals closest to them using this malevolent force. These forces of evil typically operate during the hours of the night. They are strategic in their plans, as this period makes them less prone to being seen or observed. Most of the world is asleep at this time, and they are aware of this. Therefore, they are less likely to be noticed; this time favours their evil work. No wonder our great example, Jesus, stated:

"Every day I was with you in the temple courts, and you did not lay a hand on me. But this is your hour when darkness reigns."

✦——— Luke 22:53

The Galatians were asked a question by the Apostle:

"Who hath bewitched you, that ye should not obey the truth, before whose eyes Jesus Christ hath been evidently set forth, crucified among you?"

✦——— Galatians 3:1

Why are These Agents
So Successful?

Their minds are beguiled, that is, they are unable to reason intelligently. Thus, an illusion continually leads them away from purity. The spiritual eyesight is blurred, and people who were once of untainted morals become confused under the deceptive influence of those agents of Satan who profess to be messengers of light. It is this fraudulence that gives these agents power. One may wonder why they do not come out in the open. Should they boldly reveal their intentions, they would be warded off without a moment's hesitation. They are careful to work first to obtain empathy and secure confidence in themselves as holy, self-sacrificing representatives of God. These special messengers and agents of the devil then begin their devious work of drawing away souls from the path of nobleness by attempting to make void the law of God. "For this cause [not receiving the love of the truth], God shall send them strong delusion, that they should believe a lie: that they all might be damned who believed not the truth, but had pleasure in unrighteousness" (2 Thessalonians 2:10-12). — Ellen G. White (from Testimonies for the Church, Volume 5, pages 137-148).

To overcome negative patterns and dismantle satanic operations and wickedness in one's life, it is imperative to understand the powerful strategy of midnight prayers. Unlike many in Christendom, the kingdom of darkness understands this method very well. No wonder they are so successful in utilizing this strategic time to destroy lives. They understand that their success lies in this particular time of the night, a time of vulnerability. It is a time when evil exchanges can occur— exchanging life for death. She took what was not hers—it was not her son. That is stealing. It was at midnight that this evil transaction took place.

How Midnight Prayer Destroys
the Enemy's Camp

The Christian household that prays regularly at midnight will always be an overcomer. The enemy fears believers who know how to strategize. The prayers of fervent believers are destructive to the kingdom of darkness. For those who are engaged in midnight battle, do it well. Wage good warfare. The enemy will gain the upper hand over those who are hindered by the spirit of slumber. The enemy enjoys when Christian soldiers are asleep on the battlefield. It is not easy, but it is worth it. Some may ask if this is practical to do every night. I encourage you to set realistic goals. Start by praying for one to two hours with your household. If not every night, then at least two or three nights per week.

As you get accustomed to praying at this time, the Holy Spirit will alert you of imminent dangers. Be assured that you will begin to see what is occurring in the realms of the spirit. God will begin to reveal to you the secret of your life.

What you will recognize is that your spiritual eyes will now be opened. In other words, you become your own personal prophet. Prayer at this time will now become your way of life. The closer you grow to God, the more Satan will tempt you. Do not be alarmed if, when praying, the adversary suggests weird or evil thoughts. Refocus quickly. This is nothing more than a distraction, since the enemy fears prayer and knows how devastating it will be to his territory. Ensure that you are not only in the room but in the realm.

As believers, we are expected to go through tribulations, to experience darkness in our lives, orchestrated by the kingdom of darkness because of our rejection of Satan and our decision to follow Christ. The enemy is unable to get to Christ hence the attack is against Christ's followers. "If yuh can't ketch Quaco, yuh ketch him shut." Meaning, If the person that is wanted is unreachable, then vengeance may be taken upon his relatives and followers.

The dark periods in life are formation periods in the Christian's spiritual journey. It is necessary for us to know the strategies to prevail. Engaging in midnight prayer will determine if you sink or rise, if you stay on the mountain or remain in your valley experiences. When experiencing darkness in your life, it is not time to give up. It is time to discern and to fight with the Word in prayer. Doing so during the midnight period is still one of the most effective strategies.

The Burden of Loneliness

When the enemy is attacking, it can be a lonely time for those being attacked, especially at night when sleep seems distant. It is not easy when experiencing crucibles. Who really enjoys feeling pain? Does God isolate you before He elevates you? I firmly believe so. One may think that everything is falling apart in their lives, but during this pruning season, the opposite is occurring. Everything is actually falling into place. The good news is the night season can be shortened, and daybreak can come sooner if we know how to strategically engage in midnight prayer.

Focus. Know Why You Are Up Praying

You must activate your faith in order to pray in the night season. To keep you focused on the task, it is important to know why you are up praying when everyone else is sleeping. Let the "why" be clear. Why am I fighting in prayer? What do I hope to achieve? This is because I want back everything the enemy has stolen from me. I want my enemies to be exposed, the marital delay to be overturned, and restoration of finances. I want to overcome this debt that is weighing me down. Most importantly, I do not want my children to suffer the same fate as I did through lack of knowledge. Have reasons why you are travailing in prayer. This is praying with revelation and praying intentionally. The "why" is what will push us to pray.

Jacob saw blessings in Abraham and Isaac but not in his own life. His continued request of the angel—"I will not let you go until you bless me and release my breakthrough"—is what it means to hold on to the promises of God and what God has said concerning your life. With determined faith, you fight for your destiny.

Jacob was dealing with spirits and with men. Hence the need for his wrestling. So forceful was the struggle that his hip socket was broken (Genesis 32:25). Similarly, you wrestle for your health, career, and family until you testify. It is imperative to use the spiritual weapons at the midnight hour for victory:

+ The name of Jesus (Proverbs 18:10)
+ The blood of Jesus (Revelation 12:11)
+ The fire of God (Isaiah 66:15)
+ The angels of God (Psalm 91:10-11)
+ The efficacy of the Word (Hebrews 4:12)

Preparation for Praying in the Midnight Season

———————+———————

Prepare your Heart:
The importance of this cannot be overstated. Before praying, ensure you prepare your heart to receive from God. A prepared heart is more receptive to opportunities. Prayer is a two way communication. Listen in His presence. Ask God to bring to your attention any unconfessed sins. Repent of any sin, and seek His forgiveness. Prayer is a dialogue not a monologue after

communication: Prayer is potent. It invokes the heavens to invade the earth. It can cause the supernatural to invade the natural. It creates the atmosphere for miracles.

Rest during the day

This helps keep you alert during prayer. In the same way, it is not okay to talk to your best friend half asleep. We do not want to come to the Heavenly Father with a sleepy face. Having others check in is helpful for accountability.

Cover Yourself With The Blood of Jesus

Cover yourself with the blood of Jesus. The untainted blood of Jesus cancels the attacks of the enemy. Put on the full armour of God (Ephesians 6:10-18).

Pray in the Name of Jesus

It is the access code to the throne room. It is by His name that we have access to the Father. "I will do anything you ask the Father in my name" (John 14:13).

Pray the Word

This is praying with Scriptures. At no time did Jesus tell Satan that He was the Son of God. He authoritatively told him, "It is written," and the devil had to flee. Praying without the Word is a waste of time. Since we are in battle, we need a sword. "The Word of God is powerful, like a two-edged sword" (Hebrews 4:12). For every situation one experiences, there is a Scripture. Therefore, find scriptures that are related to your situation and pray God's promises back to Him.

He admonishes us to "put Him in remembrance, pleading together so that He might be justified" (Isaiah 43:26).

Pray with Expectation

"He that comes to God must believe that He is a rewarder of those who diligently seek Him" (Hebrews 11:6). As you come into His presence, believe that your prayers will be heard. Pray, believe, and receive (Mark 11:24). Had Joseph not been in position, he would have missed his time of opportunity. For example, if you are actively job hunting, it is expected that you will start seeking out daycare services for your children so that whenever the job is ready, there will be no hindrances to your acceptance.

Persevere in Prayer:

Resist the urge to give up. During the waiting period, it is easy to believe that God is not hearing your prayers and the tendency is to fall into temptation. Some prayer requests may take years to be answered. However, trust that the all-knowing God sees and knows your pain. We should endure in prayer. Focusing while going through trials is never easy. Readers are encouraged to keep their eyes on the end goal. Keep praying until you have your evidence. While waiting, shift the weight onto Him. Hannah demonstrated great perseverance and was rewarded in the end. The same God who rewarded Hannah for her faithfulness will reward you too. We must pray without ceasing, as the Bible admonishes (1 Thessalonians 5:17). It is through faith that we grow and mature in Christ. Pray these prayers repeatedly during the midnight season to bring about victory.

Resist The Devil

Often we know that specific trials in our lives are the work of the adversary. A cry is made to God to rebuke the enemy and change our situations for the better. Are we aware that the instruction from God is for us to rebuke the enemy ourselves? "Submit to God, resist the devil, and he will flee from you" (James 4:7). As we can see, the authority over the devil is ours. We are tasked with this responsibility. The instruction did not say to have someone else resist the devil on our behalf. God has given us the authority to do so. We cannot, however, resist the devil if we do not submit to God. The law of petition is that we must stand in righteousness of Christ to be heard. We do not walk in the flesh but in the spirit.

What causes the hand of God to be displayed in the life of believers is obedience. To obey God is to act in accordance with His Word, which is His instruction. Obedience is an action word. We submit by being totally obedient to His precepts. To resist, we must first submit; thereafter, we are in a position to resist the devil, and we can expect that he will flee from us. Many believers have posited that they tried to do something, yet it did not work for them as it did for others. The key to success is to study God's Word and clothe yourself in its teachings on authority. It is very important to have God's Word built up in our spirit.

I do not know in which area of your life you are chained spiritually or who needs answers to their many mysteries in life —whether it is a financial prison, an emotional or psychological prison, a relational prison, or a spiritual prison, which is by far the worst. Midnight prayer and praise will certainly shatter those chains. Not only will it initiate the earthquake of deliverance, but it will set you free from the chains that have you bound.

I want you to understand this mystery of Midnight Prayer, which is Power. In Matthew 25:6, "And at midnight there was a cry made, Behold the bridegroom cometh; go ye out to meet him." Midnight is the time for all believers to continually assess their spiritual lives because Jesus, the bridegroom, may come in an hour unknown and unexpected—even at midnight. From the information gained from this book, use it to remind yourself and others that whatever storm of life has struck your destiny, causing you to roam about aimlessly, you have an advantage by praying strategic, Word-based prayers to shift your destiny and cancel demonic assignments against your life. When you begin to connect to the mystery of Midnight Prayer, whatever you are seeking—business, marriage, health, academics—when you connect at midnight, things begin to happen. Taking authority in prayer is announcing to the kingdom of darkness that any power of the night that is stealing from you, robbing you, afflicting you with illness, or causing unexplained delay or rejection may be destroyed in Jesus' name as you unleash and tap into the Mystery of Midnight Prayer.

The Bible records that Jacob was left alone, and a man wrestled with him until daybreak. This tells us that Jacob was left alone during the night, and Jacob wrestled with the man at the peak of the darkness. The darkness was fierce (Genesis 32:24-26). Night comes before daybreak. Needless to say, the battle becomes intense during the night season. The night season is a season of tears. It is a season of "enough is enough." Midnight prayer allows you to take a stand to shift your destiny so that your day of testimony and answered prayer will break forth. The plan of God is to grant the desires of His children (Psalm 20:4).

How to Remain Victorious

Believers are encouraged to take advantage of praying during the midnight season. By praying Scripture-based prayers with understanding, the enemy cannot defeat them. Absolutely nothing that the enemy throws their way should defeat those who are anchored in Christ. The recipe for this success is to be spiritually aware, discerning, and fully armoured. The Holy Spirit, through the Apostle Paul, prayed that the people's eyes would be fully opened to realize the full provision made for their safety. The various parts of this armour serve as protection for the believer. The responsibility of the believer is to ensure that the armour is securely fastened at all times. We are admonished to take action against the devil. The Apostle Paul writes, "Neither give place to the devil" (Ephesians 4:27).

The Importance of the Armour

* **The Waistband of Truth:** Illustrates a thorough understanding of God's Word. Similar to a soldier's belt, it secures the rest of the armour in place. Spend time in the Word.

✦ **Breastplate of Righteousness:** This has two applications. First, we put on Jesus as our righteousness. Second, it represents our obedience to the Word of God. We must stand in His righteousness to be heard.

✦ **Shod Your Feet with the Gospel of Peace:** This represents a faithful ministry proclaiming the Word of God.

✦ **Shield of Faith:** This covers the entire body, representing our complete safety under the blood of Christ, making it difficult for the enemy to break through.

✦ **Helmet of Salvation:** Represents the hope of salvation. This is the only helmet that can protect the mind, especially in these last days when many turn from the truth.

✦ **Sword of the Spirit (The Word of God):** Unlike the other parts of the armour, which are used defensively, the Word of God is used offensively. The sword, which is the Word of God, is an active weapon. The soldier of Christ, dressed in the armour of God, is well-prepared to withstand the enemy's assault (Ephesians 6:10-17).

What Was the Midnight Cry?

In His parable of the ten virgins, Christ says, "At midnight there was a cry made, Behold, the bridegroom cometh; go ye out to meet him" (Matthew 25:6). "It is in a crisis that one's character is truly revealed. There was an earnest voice proclaimed at midnight, 'Behold, the bridegroom cometh; go ye out to meet him.'" The sleeping virgins were roused from their slumbers. It was evident who had made preparations for the bridegroom's arrival. Both parties were taken by surprise, but one group was prepared for the emergency, while the other was clearly without preparation. Hence, sudden and unprepared calamity—something that brings the soul face to face with death—will show whether there is real faith in the promises of God. It will show whether the soul is sustained by grace. The great final test comes at the close of human probation, when it will be too late for the soul's need to be supplied" (Christ's Object Lessons, 412).

"With mighty power, the cry is to be sounded in our large centres of population: 'Behold, the Bridegroom cometh; go ye out to meet Him'" (Medical Ministry, p. 331). The coming of the Lord is near. As we near the close of earth's history, perils and dangers are thickening around us. Merely hearing the Word will not suffice. A life of prayer allows us to have a living connection with God. You may imagine that midnight is the darkest time of day and the least likely time for a bridegroom to arrive at a wedding. Jesus said, "I am going to prepare a place for you, and if I go to prepare a place for you, I will come again and receive you unto myself; that where I am there you will be also" (John 14:2-3). Jesus will come when we least expect it.

To many, the bridegroom, Jesus Christ, seems delayed. This delay caused the ten virgins to fall asleep as they awaited His arrival. Then suddenly, a midnight cry was heard, and the virgins started to prepare. Five of the virgins showed wisdom by bringing extra oil, which represents the Holy Spirit. The foolish virgins stated that their lamps were going out, meaning they had oil in their lamps, but it was not sufficient. The oil that was in their lamps was what they thought they needed. These foolish virgins did the bare minimum—only what they thought was necessary—and received only the minimum of the Spirit of God. Believers must pray, fast and remain in the Word to have spiritual insight and discern the evil that creeps in our midst secretly, even through those who profess our faith.

Both sets of wedding guests—the ten virgins—are believers and Christians. This suggests that both groups are Christian believers. Many would think that the wise are believers and the foolish are non-believers, but this is not the case. Jesus refers to two groups within the body of Christ that will exist at the close of earth's history. One group will gather all the oil, representing the Holy Spirit, that they can. In other words, they are not just churchgoers—they are full-time, committed Christians who strive to emulate Christ through the indwelling of the Holy Spirit. The others, the foolish, are believers who accept the Holy Spirit but not fully. They are part-time Christians, only doing what they believe is enough to be saved. These are self-righteous individuals who believe they have done enough to earn their way into the Kingdom of God. Many have created their own standards of righteousness and, as a result, have utterly failed to meet the Bible's standard. Irrespective of their high claims, they are strangers to the covenant of promise.

"For not knowing about God's righteousness and seeking to establish their own, they did not subject themselves to the righteousness of God."

— Roman 10:3

The Believer's Authority

Is there an authority we have that we are not utilizing? As believers in Christ, we have authority on this earth. Many believers, however, are yet to use this power. Many believers are merely at the edge of such authority. There are some believers who, just before Jesus comes again, will take up this authority that has always been theirs and do the work that God intended.

"And afterward, I will pour out my spirit on all people. Your sons and daughters will prophesy, your old men will dream dreams, your young men will see visions"

— Joel 2:28

Prayer Bullets

Pray, releasing them with aggression, repeatedly and intently for your situation: Believe that your prayers will be answered. Pray! Believe! Receive! (Mark 11:24).

★ ·I remove my name, my loved ones, ministry, business career, and all that concerns me from the death register. In this midnight season, in the name of Jesus,
I uproot every weapon orchestrated against me, and I declare they will not prosper in the name of Jesus (Isaiah 54:17).

★ ·I demolish every evil foundation in my life. I uproot inherited sickness, inherited poverty, and inherited diseases. In this midnight season, I command it all to leave right now. Evil water in my body, get out! Go! Every evil dedication in my life is cancelled in the name of Jesus (Psalm 11:3).

* In this midnight season, I take back and claim all my prosperity in the name of Jesus. I speak to and claim back every door of prosperity that has been shut; I command you now to open. Father Lord, convert every poverty in my life to prosperity, convert my mistakes to perfection, turn every frustration to fulfillment, God of impossibilities bring honey out of the rock for me in Jesus' name (3 John 1:2).

* Father, in this midnight season, I lift a battle cry of deliverance and blessings over my life. I tread upon the high places of the enemies, I annihilate and render useless every blood-sucking demon, and I command every evil stronghold in my life to lose its grip in the name of Jesus (Isaiah 49:24-26).

* Lord Jesus, in this midnight season, I stand against every evil covenant of sudden death. I break every conscious and unconscious evil covenant of untimely death sent against my life. You spirit of death and hell, depart from my life in the name of Jesus (Psalm 118:17).

* Warring angels of God, smash every satanic bank where my finances have been diverted in the spirit world. Let them be destroyed by the earthquake of the Lord in Jesus' name (Joshua 1:8).

- In this midnight season, Blood of Jesus, cry against every evil gathering against my life. Convert all my past failures to unlimited victories, in the name of Jesus (Isaiah 54:15-17).

- Every demonic limitation of my progress that is threatening shame, in this midnight season, be removed. I paralyze every network of shame around me. Those who seek my shame shall be ashamed for my sake; I will not record any point for Satan as far as shame is concerned (Romans 10:11-15).

- All evil counsellors and conspirators gathering this night against my destiny, be scattered! Let the rain of fire fall upon every hardened enemy of my destiny in Jesus' name (Micah 5:9).

- King of glory, any evil friend or member of my household hiding under a masquerade to attack my life, my marriage, my career, or my destiny, be exposed, we arrest you and drag you to the Court of Heaven for sentencing in Jesus' name (Matthew 10:36 & Psalm 41:9).

- Mighty God, every evil wind blowing the blessings of God away from me, backfires in the name of Jesus (Proverbs 21:21).

- I recover all my money stolen from me spiritually or physically in Jesus' name. Powers fighting against answers to my prayers, receive the judgment of death in Jesus' name (Joel 2:25-26).

- I declare that I am divinely insured against calamity, sudden sickness, untimely death, and every form of tragedy in the name of Jesus (Psalm 140:4).

- Warring angels, arise by fire! Track down all the powers planning to attack me in my dreams or in the physical realm, in Jesus' name (Proverbs 3:24).

- I flush out every poison, every sickness, and disease planted in my body from evil consumption in dreams, I bring the hook of the Lord against every dream manipulator in Jesus' name. (Mark 16:18).

- O Lord, make my prayers crash land with paralyzing force and terrorize the enemies of my destiny in Jesus' name (Matthew 7:7-8).

- I destroy every satanic parasite, worm, maggot, and leech attached to my finances. O Lord, arise, set me free, and set my enemies against each other in Jesus' name (Malachi 3:11-12).

- Every power that puts marriages asunder shall not prosper in my home. Spirits of lust assigned against my marriage will not work; unforgiving spirits will not prosper in my home in Jesus' name. I soak my marriage and family in the blood of Jesus (Ephesians 5:33).

- Mighty Conqueror, your Holy Spirit bears witness with me that I am Your child and a joint-heir with Christ Jesus. I am more than a conqueror because you love me (Romans 8:16-17, 29).

- Father Lord, in the same way that Abraham sent his servant to fetch a wife for his son Isaac, wherever my purpose partner is trapped, send the Holy spirit to bring the bone of my bones and flesh of my flesh to me in the name of Jesus (Genesis 24:4).

- I command all adversaries of my breakthrough to be put to shame. I am endowed with the power to excel among all competitors; I am the head and not the tail, above and not beneath (Psalm 25:3).

- Mighty Warrior, build a hedge of protection around the heart, eyes, and ears of my husband—that anything meant for foolishness, lust, be kept and ignored—in the name of Yeshua. He will bring me good not harm every day of his life (Eph. 3:5).

- It is you Lord who delivers me from my powerful enemies and sets me free from those who are too strong for me. (Psalm 18:17).

- All my children shall be taught of the Lord. They will not be at the wrong place at the wrong time. They will not die before their time; they will not receive battles packaged as blessings. They will know their Creator and will do mighty exploits for their King (Psalm 112:2).

- Father, let my glory attract marriage in the name of Jesus. I paralyze every work of the enemy to frustrate me during courtship. I will not marry the wrong person or out of desperation. Every door to my marriage that the enemy has closed, be opened now in the name of Jesus (Ecclesiastes 4:9-10).

- Father, I cover all my studies and those of my family in the blood of Jesus. I shall not forget what to write in exams in Jesus' name. O Lord, give unto me wisdom during the exam; I arrest every spiritual robber stealing my results. I curse every spirit of academic failure; Lord, plant academic success in my life, in the name of Jesus (Col 3:23).

- Heavenly Father, empower my marriage to manifest physically. As Abraham sent his servant to fetch a wife for his son Isaac, send the Holy Spirit to locate my godly spouse in the name of Jesus. I refuse to marry out of desperation in Jesus' name (Hosea 2:19-20).

* Heavenly Father, thank you that my wife and purpose partner is a virtuous woman and more precious than rubies. Help me to trust her completely, may she greatly enrich my life. I terminate every marriage-breaking spirit. I decree she will bring me good not evil all the days of her life in Jesus name (Proverbs 31:10-12).

* Jehovah Jireh, let Kingdom prosperity flow through this business. Open the windows of Heaven and pour out so many blessings we cannot contain. Rebuke the devourer for our sake, as you promised. Provide outstanding employees who share our values and mission. Strategically position us with the right clients and suppliers. Help us to be good stewards and make this business a lighthouse in the marketplace in Jesus' name (Deuteronomy 8:18).

* Jehovah Gibbor contends with those who fight with me. Take hold of the shield and buckler stand up for my help. Draw out your spear and javelin and close up the way of my persecutors. Let them be ashamed that seek after my soul, let my mockers be put to shame. Let the devisers be turned back and brought to confusion. Let not my enemies wrongfully rejoice over me. (Psalm 35)

King of Glory, live out thy life within me. I repent of every sin knowingly and unknowingly that has given the enemy access to my life. Close any opened door. I humble myself before you. I surrender my life to you. Help me to live and walk in holiness and righteousness before You all the days of my life. May my life be an example to others. May they see Christ in me and come to glorify you whom to know is life eternal. Help me to stay and get others ready for the nearness of your coming. (James 4:10)

What Happens to Our Prayers Next

Prayer is not the power itself; it is the instrument that grants us access to the power. The Godhead is the true source of this power. After we battle in prayer, our petitions leave us, and as they ascend to Heaven, they are placed before the throne of God in the twenty-four golden bowls surrounding it. The elders deliver our prayers to the Holy Spirit, who then presents them to Jesus. He interprets our prayers according to Heaven's language, ascribing new meaning to them (which is why we pray in the name of Jesus). As our Advocate, He receives our prayers, blesses and sanctifies them, mediates on our behalf, and makes our requests worthy to go before the Father. The Father then releases the power of intervention to fix, change, eradicate, overrule, annul, prosper, break protocols, provide answers, bring deliverance, breakthroughs, healing, and grant the desires of our hearts.

"And I will do whatever you ask in my name, so that the Father may be glorified in the Son."

✦—— John 14:13

CHAPTER 6

CONCLUSION

As you read this book, the contents therein are life-changing. Be reminded that the blood of Jesus is thicker than water. Do not forget that we were crucified with Him. targeted prayer, fasting and praise are lethal weapons in the hands of believers. When used strategically, they demolish strongholds. Believers should always be reminded that our future is preordained and destined by God, and each of us has been given a colourful destiny. The adversary of our souls has redesigned the destiny of many, causing them to rethink their existence. Praying during the midnight season is a great method to realign your destiny with God's original plan.

"I wish above all things that you prosper and be in good health even as thy soul prospers".

— John 3:2

It is God's desire that His children prosper and be in good health to enjoy such prosperity. Perhaps yours has been shifted by the kingdom of darkness; take it back through the medium of strategic prayer. I give blessings and add no sorrow. (Proverbs 10:22). Our lives and the lives of our family are in HIS hands. As we await the coming of Jesus, He told us to occupy until He comes. Let us pray authoritatively, utilizing the midnight prayer strategy and shifting things back into perspective, reclaiming all the enemy has stolen in Jesus' name.

The enemy has held you hostage for too long. Satan has no legal right to dominate or rule us. The debt is already paid by Jesus who took those thirty-nine stripes mercilessly for us. It is therefore impossible for us to be recharged for a ransom that is already paid in full. At the Cross of Calvary, Jesus declared it is finished; at no time did He say we are finished. His blood paid it all. The enemy whose only intent is to steal, kill and destroy must be challenged with these facts through the medium of prayer. Some Christians, through fear, seem to have more faith in the tricks and authority of the devil than in the power God has given us.

Have you had enough? Do not allow the enemy to beat you black and blue or reduce you to crumbs anymore. Put an end to it today.

"Whatever things you disallow on earth are disallowed by heaven, and whatever you authorize on earth is authorized by heaven."

— Matthew 18:18

Jesus is coming soon. Believers should not expect the days ahead of us to get easier. In fact, this is contrary to Scripture. For in the last days there will be perilous times. Such things must happen but the end is not yet. (Matthew 24). This means we still have to occupy until our Saviour comes. The adversary of our souls realizes that he has but a short time. Furthermore, the enemy recognizes that paradise is forever lost where it is concerned. Why? The enemy had it lost it and can't regain it. Knowing this, the enemy will not make it easy for us knowing what those who are totally surrendered to Christ will inherit. Midnight prayers train us to fight in prayer. We have a part to play in our salvation. To anchor our faith as the hope of Jesus' return burns in our hearts. It will not be an honorary victory. Only those who endure to the end will be saved in God's eternal Kingdom.

With holy anger in that midnight season, engage the service of the blood of Jesus against the happenings of the enemy in your lives, home, and environment. Using this time of prayer, redirect the enemy to the potency of the blood. The blood of Jesus speaks mercy for the saints, but that very same blood speaks judgment for the sinner. Jesus' blood is the legal system that breaks every accusation of the enemy against us.

Make the sacrifice; pray targeted prayers during the night season. Victory is assured for you and your loved ones. You have authority over the devil. No matter how hard the enemy is fighting, as you fight in prayer, wielding the weapons of your warfare, it will send that old dragon packing. As the prayers ascend, the Holy Spirit hands over our prayers to Father who places them in the golden bowl, examines our request and releases the answer to us. We serve a victorious Creator not the creature. We will not sell out, we will not quit. Engage in midnight prayer to seal your victory.

We are overcomers! The enemy lost badly before yet still desires a re-match. Will be beaten again. Do not be intimidated! The power is on the inside of you. Take authority! **Exercise it!.**

ABOUT THE AUTHOR

SHERENE A.P. BROWN (C.P.S., B.A., M.A., M.S., Ed.) is an ardent Christian who loves the Lord wholeheartedly and believes in the power that lies within prayer. She has a firm belief that the Ten Commandments are the platform set by God for His children to live in worship, obedience, praise, and adoration to Him in preparation for His imminent return.

She believes that soldiers in God's army should be rightly trained to effectively release the weapons of prayer and fasting in the enemy's camp to get answers to their prayers. She has a burning desire to see God's people reach a place of intensified prayer and fasting and firmly believes that with such weaponry, God's people will not only dislodge but also severely interrupt satanic forces and gain victory against the adversary.

Through experiential knowledge, prayer counseling sessions, personal interactions and observation, she has witnessed the destructive forces of the enemy against God's children. She has also coached and seen many lives transformed through the strategic use of the weapons of prayer, fasting, and praise. She enjoys reading, traveling, meeting people, teaching, preaching the Word of God, and leading prayer conferences and retreats.

She is an educator, motivational speaker, and prayer leader, and is experienced in the fields of philosophy, counseling, business, and education. However, her passion lies in teaching the intricacies of prayer. She is the core founder of Global Midnight Prayer Ministry, a midnight warfare prayer ministry that brings like-minded believers from across the globe to pray. She holds Isaiah 43:2 close to her heart:

"When you pass through the waters, I will be with you; and through the rivers, they shall not overflow you. When you walk through the fire, you shall not be burned, nor shall the flames scorch you."

Thank you for reading. If this book has blessed and enlightened you, please consider leaving an honest review on your favourite store.

Stay tuned for more topics coming soon!

NOTES

NOTES

NOTES

NOTES

NOTES

NOTES

NOTES

NOTES

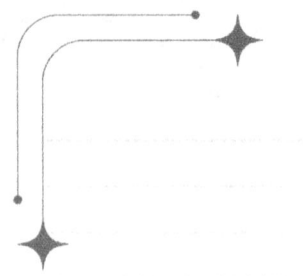

NOTES

NOTES